Doctors

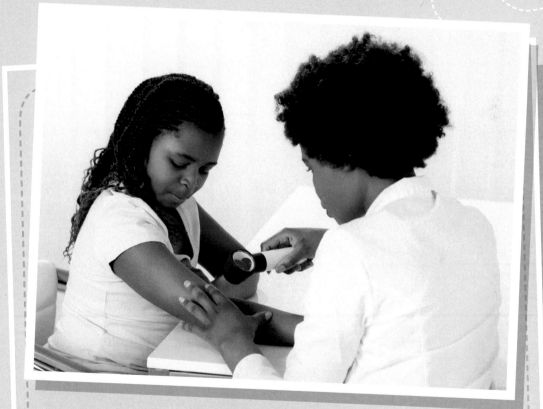

Izzi Howell

W

FRANKLIN WATTS

LONDON•SYDNEY

Franklin Watts
First published in Great Britain in 2018 by The Watts Publishing Group
Copyright © The Watts Publishing Group, 2018

Produced for Franklin Watts by
White-Thomson Publishing Ltd
www.wtpub.co.uk

ISBN: 978 1 4451 6493 9
10 9 8 7 6 5 4 3 2 1

Credits
Series Editor: Izzi Howell
Series Designer: Rocket Design (East Anglia) Ltd
Designer: Clare Nicholas
Literacy Consultant: Kate Ruttle

The publisher would like to thank the following for permission to reproduce their pictures: Getty: sturti cover, SolStock 4, PeopleImages 6, RichLegg 7, fstop123 9, FatCamera 10, Adie Bush 11b, KidStock 13t, Bigandt_ Photography 15b, ERproductions Ltd 17, monkeybusinessimages 18b, Digital Vision 21; Shutterstock: Andrey_ Popov title page and 20, Image Point Fr 5, Monkey Business Images 8, 16 and 19, Alexander Raths 11t, Suzanne Tucker 12, Slava_kovtun 13b, Africa Studio 14t, ANURAK PONGPATIMET 15 and 12, wavebreakmedia 18t.

Every attempt has been made to clear copyright. Should there be any inadvertent omission please apply to the publisher for rectification.

Printed in China

Franklin Watts
An imprint of
Hachette Children's Group
Part of The Watts Publishing Group
Carmelite House
50 Victoria Embankment
London EC4Y 0DZ

An Hachette UK Company
www.hachette.co.uk
www.franklinwatts.co.uk

MIX
Paper from
responsible sources
FSC® C104740

All words in **bold** appear in the glossary on page 23.

Contents

Who are doctors?

Doctors help people who are ill or hurt. They find out what is wrong. Then they try to make the person better.

▲ This doctor is testing this man's **blood pressure** to find out why he feels ill.

Doctors work in **doctors' surgeries** or in hospitals.

Some doctors wear white coats. Other doctors just wear their normal clothes. ▶

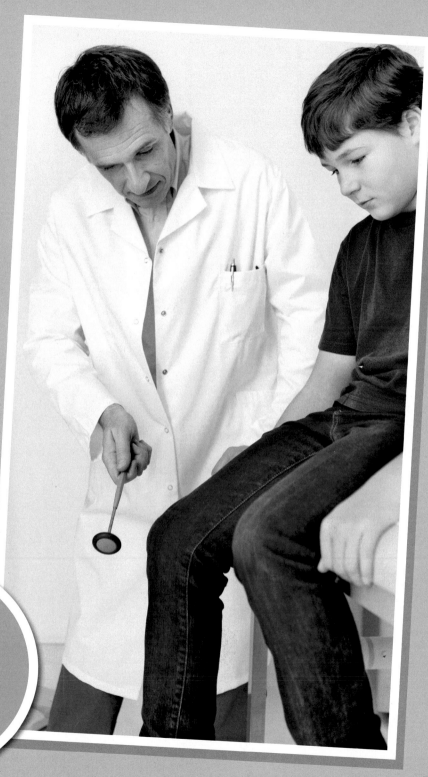

When was the last time you talked to a doctor?

Making an appointment

You usually need to make an **appointment** to see a doctor. You can make an appointment by contacting the doctors' surgery.

◀ This woman is ill so she is phoning to make an appointment to see a doctor.

When you arrive at the doctors' surgery, you should tell the **receptionist** that you have an appointment. Then, you sit in the waiting room until the doctor is ready to see you.

This boy and his mother are letting the receptionist know that they have arrived for their appointment. ▼

The appointment

During an appointment, the doctor talks to the **patient**. He or she will ask the patient what's wrong.

▼ This girl is telling the doctor that she has a cough.

What questions do you think doctors ask their patients?

Sometimes, doctors need to **examine** a patient. They look at the patient's body to see what the problem is.

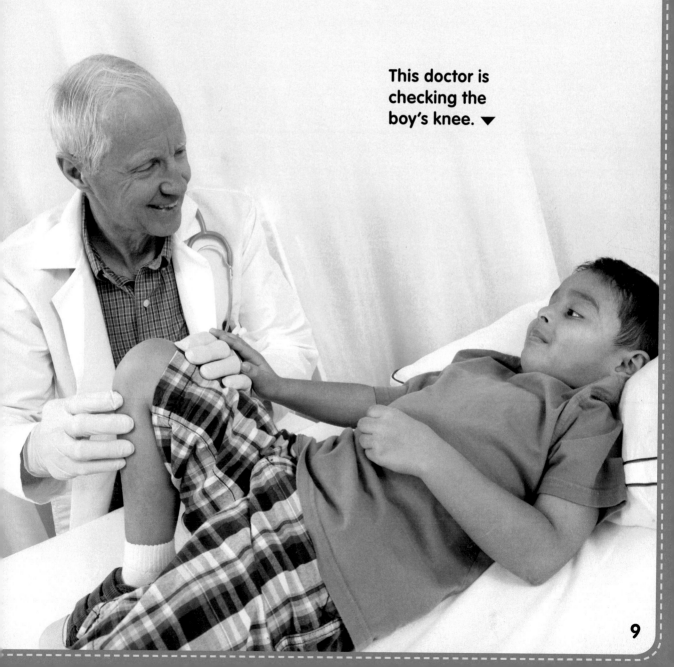

This doctor is checking the boy's knee. ▼

Instruments

Doctors use different **instruments** to examine a patient. They use a **stethoscope** to hear inside the body.

A doctor listens to your heartbeat and your breathing with a stethoscope. ▼

stethoscope

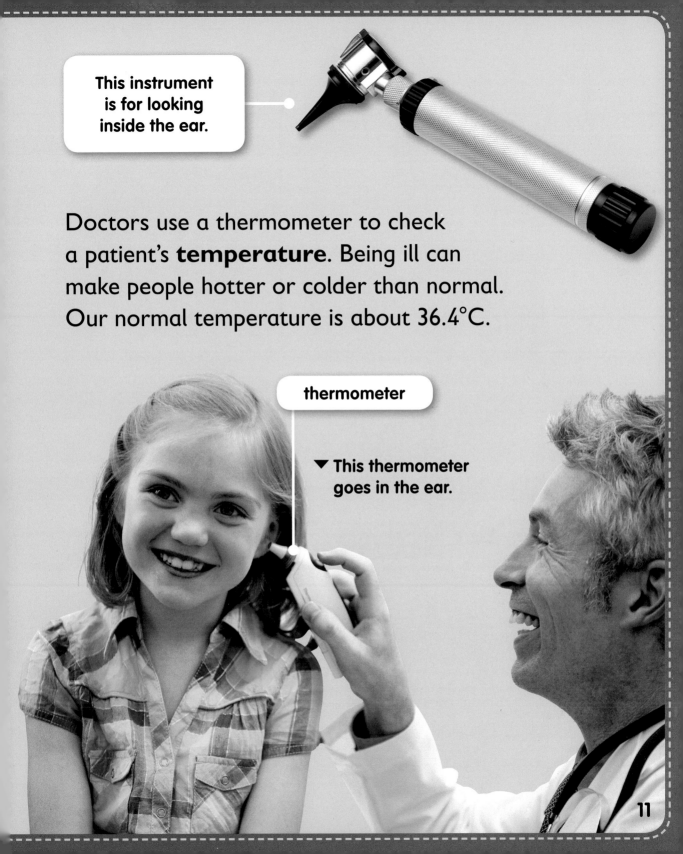

This instrument is for looking inside the ear.

Doctors use a thermometer to check a patient's **temperature**. Being ill can make people hotter or colder than normal. Our normal temperature is about 36.4°C.

thermometer

▼ This thermometer goes in the ear.

Getting better

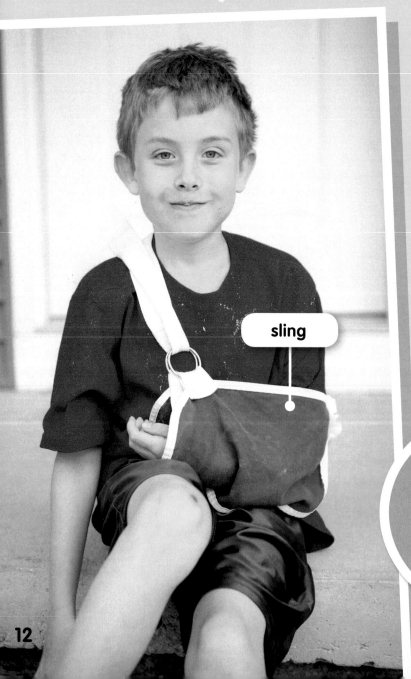

sling

When a doctor knows what is wrong with a patient, they try to help them get better.

◀ The doctor told this boy to rest his hurt arm in a sling until it has healed.

Have you ever worn a sling before? Why?

◀ If you take the prescription to a pharmacy, they will give you your medicine.

If you are ill, you might need to take medicine to feel better. The doctor will give you a **prescription**.

Some medicines are pills. Others come as liquids.
▼

Only take medicine that an adult gives to you.

Good health

▲ Sleeping is very important for your health.

Being **healthy** stops you from becoming ill as often. Eating fruit and vegetables and doing exercise help to keep you healthy.

◀ Brushing your teeth will keep your mouth healthy.

Keeping clean also helps to stop illnesses. It's important to wash your hands after using the toilet. You should also wash them before you eat.

◀ You should cover your nose when you sneeze. This stops other people from catching your illness.

Accident and emergency

People go to hospital if they are very ill or hurt themselves badly. Doctors **treat** these patients in the **A&E (accident and emergency) department**.

Lots of doctors and nurses work together in A&E to help people feel better quickly. ▼

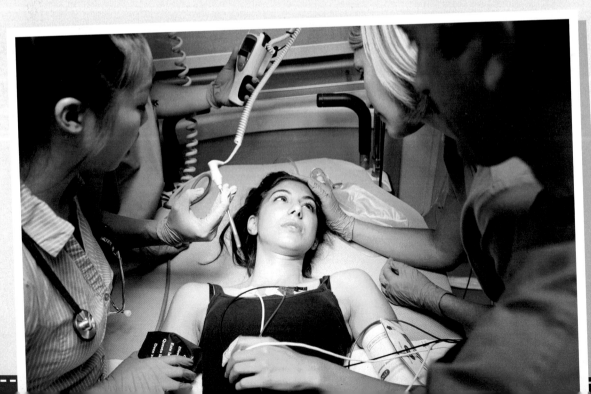

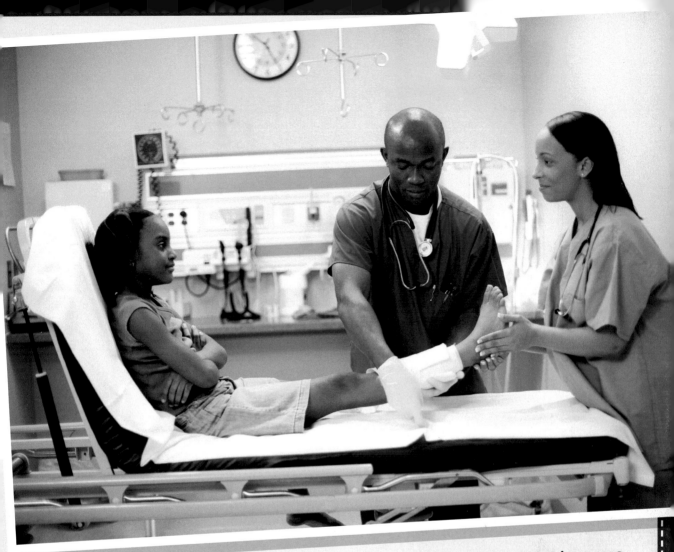

▲ This girl is in A&E because she has broken her leg. Once it is wrapped in a **cast**, she can go home.

You might need to go to A&E if you bump your head hard or have a deep cut. People also go to A&E if they break a bone.

Have you ever broken a bone? Which bone was it?

Staying in hospital

If a patient is very ill or hurt, they might need to stay in hospital. Sometimes, they stay in a bed on a **ward** with other patients.

▲ These children are on the same ward.

This girl has her own hospital room. ▶

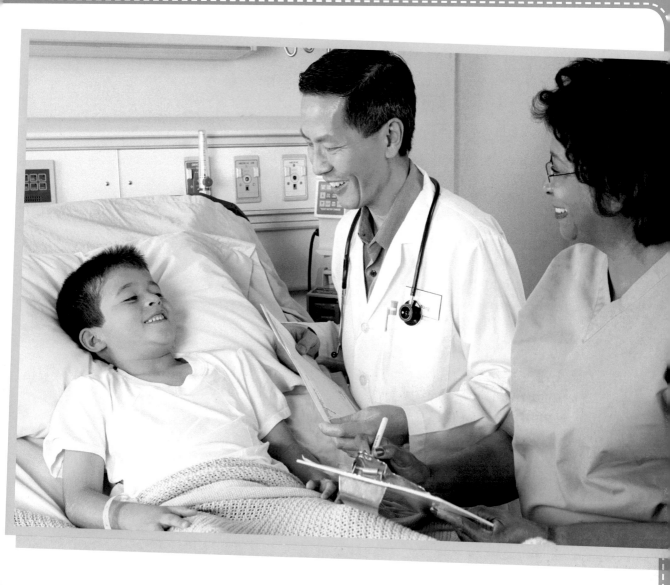

Doctors check on patients
in hospital to see how they
are feeling. Patients have
to stay until they are better.
Then they can go home.

▲ This hospital doctor
is asking this boy
how he feels.

Specialists

Sometimes, patients need to see a specialist. Specialists are doctors who know a lot about one disease or one part of the body.

A skin specialist is looking at this girl's arm. ▼

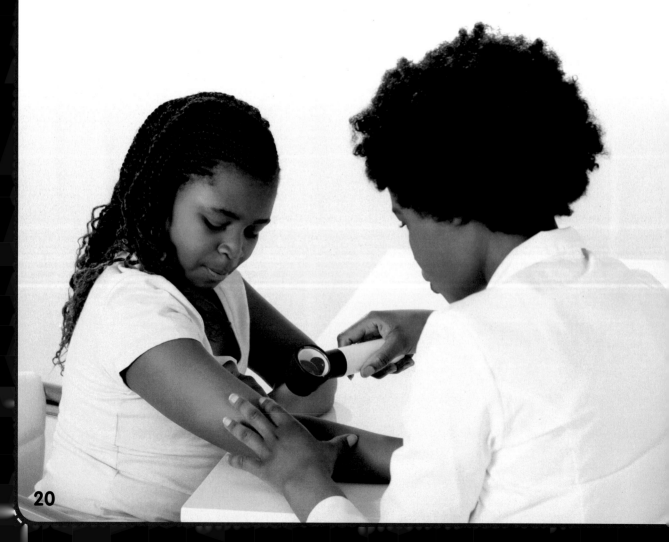

Some specialists treat people with stomach problems. Other specialists help people who can't hear well.

This boy has breathing problems. The specialist is checking how well he can blow.

▼

How hard can you blow?

Quiz

Test how much you remember.

Check your answers on page 24.

1 How can you make a doctor's appointment?

2 What happens when a doctor examines a patient?

3 What is a stethoscope for?

4 Where should you take a prescription to get your medicine?

5 Why do people go to A&E?

6 What is a specialist?

Glossary

A&E (accident and emergency) department – the part of a hospital that treats people with serious problems as soon as they arrive

appointment – an agreed time and place to visit someone

blood pressure – the strength at which blood moves around the body

cast – a hard cover used to keep a broken bone in place until it heals

doctors' surgery – a place where doctors work and see patients

examine – to look at something carefully

healthy – strong and well

instrument – a tool

patient – someone who is being cared for by a doctor

prescription – a piece of paper that says which medicine someone needs to take

receptionist – someone who helps visitors in a place such as a doctors' surgery

stethoscope – an instrument used to hear inside the body

temperature – how hot or cold someone or something is

treat – to try to make better someone who is hurt or ill

ward – a room with several beds where people stay in a hospital

Index

Answers:

1: By ringing the doctors' surgery; 2: The doctor looks at the patient's body to see what's wrong;
3: To hear inside the body; 4: A pharmacy; 5: Because they are very ill or have hurt themselves badly;
6: A doctor who knows a lot about one disease or part of the body

Teaching notes:

Children who are reading Book band Gold or above should be able to enjoy this book with some independence. Other children will need more support.

Before you share the book:

- Talk about children's prior knowledge and experience of doctors, emphasising their role in keeping people healthy.

- Check that children have a good understanding of feeling well/ unwell.

- If any children have a disability or chronic health condition such as diabetes or asthma, invite them to share their experiences of how doctors try to keep them well.

While you share the book:

- Help children to read some of the more unfamiliar words.

- Talk about the questions. Encourage children to make links between their own experiences and the information in the book.

- Discuss the pictures, talking about what the doctors are doing and why. Talk about the equipment they are using.

- Talk about doctors in your locality. Where are the local surgeries? Do children know where the nearest hospital is?

After you have shared the book:

- If possible, take children to visit a doctors' surgery out of hours, or invite a doctor to come and talk to the class.

- Make a poster of things we can all do to keep well and healthy.

- Work through the free activity sheets at www.hachetteschools.co.uk

People who help us

Doctors

978 1 4451 6493 9

Who are doctors?
Making an appointment
The appointment
Instruments
Getting better
Good health
Accident and emergency
Staying in hospital
Specialists

Firefighters

978 1 4451 6489 2

Who are firefighters?
Emergency!
Fire engines
Uniform
Rescuing people
Equipment
Trapped people
The fire station
Fire safety

Paramedics

978 1 4451 6495 3

Who are paramedics?
Emergency!
On the scene
The ambulance
Treating patients
At hospital
First responders
Air ambulances
First aid

Police Officers

978 1 4451 6491 5

Who are police officers?
Uniform
On patrol
999
The crime scene
Evidence
The police station
Vehicles
Animals

Islam

Religion

Christianity
978 1 4451 5962 1
Hinduism
978 1 4451 5964 5
Islam
978 1 4451 5968 3
Judaism
978 1 4451 5966 9

Queen Elizabeth II

History

Neil Armstrong
978 1 4451 5948 5
Queen Elizabeth II
978 1 4451 5886 0
Queen Victoria
978 1 4451 5950 8
Tim Berners-Lee
978 1 4451 5952 2

Japan

Countries

Argentina
978 1 4451 5958 4
India
978 1 4451 5960 7
Japan
978 1 4451 5956 0
The United Kingdom
978 1 4451 5954 6

FRANKLIN WATTS